Love
Cathie

Nick's Nook

North Delta's Community Action for Food Security

A United Way BC Hi Neighbour and Magical Hearts Community Initiative

FriesenPress

One Printers Way
Altona, MB R0G 0B0
Canada

www.friesenpress.com

ISBN
978-1-03-833863-1 (Hardcover)
978-1-03-833862-4 (Paperback)
978-1-03-833864-8 (eBook)

1. JUVENILE NONFICTION, VOLUNTEERING

Distributed to the trade by The Ingram Book Company

In North Delta lived a group so kind,

the Magical Hearts, with love in their mind.

They saw a need and took a stand,

to help those struggling who needed a hand.

They started a pantry, small but true,
Nick's Nook, where people could come for food.
Food and essentials, there for free,
to help them through tough times, you see.

At first, they stocked it on their own
but soon the community and neighbours had grown!
With generous donations from far and wide,
a collective effort and community pride!

Government, business and community too,
stepped up to help and provide the food.
But the Magical Hearts did not stop there,
they worked with United Way BC to build a greater share,
a partnership helping the most,
with neighbours contributing to the post.

Delta City Hall

Together, they worked to help those in need,
providing more resources than ever, indeed!
With United Way BC's support and might,
Nick's Nook shone an even brighter light.

Word spread like wildfire, you bet,
More people came, with needs to be met.
Magical Hearts and United Way BC,
worked tirelessly each and every day.

Through their love and kindness, they built a bond,
for Nick's Nook, a community and far beyond.
They inspired others to do the same,
to spread love and kindness, with no shame.

In North Delta, a magical tale,
Of how love and kindness can prevail.
Nick's Nook, a life-changing shining light,
providing comfort to all, both day and night.

TEACHER'S NOTES – NICK'S NOOK/ SPONSORED BY UNITED WAY BC

Community Cupboards and Pantries are all about neighbours helping neighbours to get the food they need when they need it. In Delta these programs are making a difference 24 hours a day, seven days a week for those with food needs and those with items to give. We're going to share with you the story of Nick's Nook and just how Community Pantries got started in our community.

A group call Magical Hearts, who are based in North Delta, started Nick's Nooks to honour the memory of Nickolas Watters by naming them after him. Nickolas was a North Delta resident who passed from lung disease at age 18, but whose life impacted many of those who knew and loved him. Magical Hearts is a group formed in 2014 with the support of the friends and families of The Society of American Magicians. The Magical Hearts group has a simple mission: to spread love, hope, and kindness throughout their community and other communities one act at a time.

During the COVID-19 pandemic, individuals from Magical Hearts noticed many families in their neighborhood were struggling to put food on their tables. During this difficult time, community members asked if the Magical Hearts could support some families with food hampers.

Partnering with United Way BC and community members, they helped several neighbourhood families. A chance encounter with a 10-year-old boy, who was so excited to receive a gallon of milk from the group, was the catalyst for Magical Hearts to make the North Delta Little Free Pantry, named Nick's Nook, a reality.

Moved by the food needs of their neighbours, the group created the first no-barrier food source in community. No barrier means individuals and families can take the food they need without judgement, stigma, or shame. The pantry is open 24 hours 7 days a week for all who need it. All pantries and cupboards are based on a "take what you need, leave what you can" philosophy and include non-perishable food, sanitary products, diapers and more.

Magical Hearts rallied with other local groups around the area. They partnered with United Way BC Hi Neighbour program and the Delta Community Foundation and built the first Nick's Nook at Northside Community Church located at 11300 84th Ave Delta. Multicultural language signs invited anyone in the community who needed food to take what they need for today and leave what they could for tomorrow.

At first, Magical Hearts stocked the pantry with items from their own cupboards, but soon, their friends, neighbors, businesses, and community organizations began to contribute.

The community quickly rallied around Nick's Nook, and before long, it had become a vital resource for families and persons in need. One pantry turned into two, with Nick's Nook 2 opening at New Hope Christian Church located at 11838 88th Avenue. The pantry was sponsored by United Way BC and other community groups and organizations.

Nick's Nook 3 followed at Sunshine Ridge Baptist Church located at 6320 120th Street, again built with support from United Way BC and community volunteers to serve another part of our neighbourhood. Nick's Nook 4, supported by United Way BC and other friends was the next community resource to be added to our North Delta neighbourhood at Crossroads Church located at 7655 120th Street in North Delta.

Magical Hearts made sure to keep the pantry stocked and always maintained. They also started to include items like toiletries and baby food. They began to organize community events, like food drives and fundraisers to raise awareness, donations and funds for their cause.

As the word spread about Nick's Nook, more and more people began to rely on it, and more and more Little Free Pantries and Community Cupboards were built, first around the Lower Mainland and Fraser Valley, then across BC.

Magical Hearts then created a community volunteer network called North Delta Small Pantry volunteers who work tirelessly to keep the pantry stocked and to aid anyone who needs it. They also began to collaborate with other organizations in their community, like food banks and homeless shelters, to provide even more resources to those in need.

Through their efforts, Magical Hearts, United Way BC, the City of Delta and many other community businesses and organizations have created more than just a pantry. They have created a community of love and compassion, where people come together to support one another during difficult times. As the pandemic receded and life started to return to normal, Nick's Nook continued to grow, spreading kindness and hope throughout BC and inspiring others to do the same. And it's all thanks to two young boys with big hearts.

At the time of publishing in early 2025, Nick's Nook has inspired 10 other Nooks across BC.

Nick's Nooks acknowledges the following supporters of our Little Free Pantry, without whom this project would not have become a reality.

SPECIAL THANKS TO:

Magical Hearts, United Way BC Hi Neighbour Program, New Hope Christian Church, Sunshine Ridge Baptist Church, Northside Community Church, Crossroads Church, The City of Delta, Mayor George Harvie and Delta City Council, Mark Johnson, Marjorie Jobling, Olga Shcerbyna, Southridge Hardware, Advantage Realty, Envision Financial, Bode Farms, Sands Secondary School, Seaquam Life Skills Class, Shannon Miller and team, Spot On Homes, Darrell Poetker Remax Performance Realty, North Delta Small Pantry Volunteers, 100 Women Who Care Fraser Valley, Sunshine Hills Community Group, North Delta Artisan and Gift Market. Delta Community Small Grants, Surrey Food Bank, Mama's to Mama's and Delta Assist, the Boag Foundation and the Rotary Club of North Delta.

Additional special thanks to the Nick's Nook Project Team, whose vision and determination brought this valuable resource to North Delta!

Monisha, Vera, Susan, Lyn, Cathie, Amanda, Daniela, Kristie, Ann and Vrindy!

Grateful thank you to Vrindy Spencer, our inspiration!

THANK *YOU* TO OUR LITTLE FREE PANTRY BUILDERS:

Jeff Ochbrect, Dave Watters, Dave Coleman, Mike Methven, and Rob Watson.

Extra special thanks to the students from six local Delta schools who were our amazing writers and illustrators of the Nick's Nook book. Their talent and enthusiasm and dedication shines through!

Emily Hatzisavva, Kyo Howard, Sage Roth, Mckenzie Wocknitz, Noah Shouchuk, Armaan Boparai, Jonah Macedo, Talya Harnik, Veer Rana, Jasper Stuchberry,

Anmol Jandu, Everly Olson, Madden Wocknitz, Angad Jandu and Cathie Watters,

HOW CAN YOU HELP?

We are always looking for sponsors or volunteers, please email NDsmallpantry@gmail.com.

Proceeds of this book will go to food security programs for Nick's Nooks!